Copyright

First Printing, 2024

PREFACE

The truth is, I fought against writing this book.

I have long been a believer that e-courses, instructional videos and books that purport to teach a specific subject are lacking a critical element: A personal touch.

If you see a video on The Golf Channel where Tiger Woods' swing coach offers to help you fix your slice for the low, low price of $1400 and a kidney, what you're getting are general tips that will help most people. Some of what's in that video is probably also insightful, inspiring and might even genuinely help you become a better golfer.

But even Tiger Woods' swing coach will tell you that to really get the most out of Tiger's potential, books and videos won't get the job done. If you look up my company on social media, you'll likely find a pinned post that reads something like this:

"Tom Brady would have thrown just as many touchdown passes if he learned about football by watching YouTube videos."

While the world's most legendary athletes, actors, musicians, chefs and business leaders have achieved great things because of a certain amount of natural aptitude, there's no question that somewhere along the way, someone took them by the metaphorical hand and guided them toward greatness.

I hope that for you, the metaphorical hand is the one that is now holding this book, and it leads to us getting together over coffee sometime (physically or virtually) to get you closer to the status of "legend" as well. If, at the end of this book, the idea of working together one-on-one is appealing, the "Afterword" section has some details on how we might do that.

You'll notice that this book has almost nothing to do with the gear you're using to actually get audio and video from your body into the eyes and ears of your audience, with the exception of Chapter 12. Our focus here is on improving the quality of your content. And with all due respect and deference to the various gurus on the interwebs, my experience has been that we all focus on the details we're most competent at executing. A show hosted by a professional podcast producer might have pristine audio, but might have gaping holes in the quality of the content.

Additionally, the types of shows we're focused on here are those based on conversations, whether that's a conversation between participants on the show, or between the host and their audience. We're not digging into audio dramas or TV series here; those productions are far beyond the scope of my expertise, though I have been asked in the past to critique performances of voice actors, which I still do from time to time.

If this is not the first time you're encountering something I've written, note that there may be echoes here of material you have read, seen or heard me say someplace else. That's not surprising, because the things I'm going to say here are things I have been saying and sharing for years. They're based on concepts that haven't changed, and won't change anytime soon. This is simply the first time I've knitted all these ideas together into something cohesive.

How to Try and Sound More Like an Announcer

Please don't.

How to Try and Sound More Like an Announcer (Pt 2)

As of this writing, it is estimated that American radio talk show host Sean Hannity has approximately 16 *million* listeners.

I would describe Sean Hannity's voice as reminding me what it's like to listen to someone who is first learning to play the bagpipes; the sound is kind of like what I imagine you would get if you threw a bunch of kittens in a bag and swung it over your head like a ceiling fan.

I *would* describe it that way, but it would be unfair.

...to the kittens.

Look, you sound the way you sound. The moment you start trying to sound different than that, is the moment you stop sounding like you.

Are there tweaks you could make to *how* you use your voice, like perhaps projecting a little more loudly, enunciating a little more carefully, or breaking free of a monotone delivery and using some variety in your range?

Sure.

But all of those things are simply tweaks to get the most out of what you already have. I've lost track of the number of people who have never started, simply because they didn't think they sounded "announcer-y enough".

If you'd like some other examples of legends behind the microphone who had voices that were less than "radio friendly", I'll point you toward people like Dr. Ruth Westheimer, who had a massive international following for her call-in show, *Sexually Speaking*, but a voice that made me think of almost anything *but* intimate relations.

Another example that springs to mind for me is comedian Steven Wright, who enjoyed massive success in the late 1980s and was ranked at #15 on a list of the Best Stand-Up Comedians of All-Time compiled by *Rolling Stone* magazine. Steven Wright had no variety in his delivery at all. The digital assistant on your phone displays a far greater range of emotion and tone. But people were riveted to what he was saying, and his voice was simply the vehicle to get his unique perspectives and ideas out into the world.

Style is temporary. Substance is forever. Give me something worth listening to, and I'll forgive the lapses in the slickness of your delivery.

What's far more important is having something worth communicating, and speaking clearly enough that I don't have to fight to understand what you're saying.

Hundreds of co-hosts, co-workers, competitors and clients later, and I've still never heard a single person who was "trying" to sound like an announcer who didn't sound fake and forced to the point where it was distracting.

Have the courage to just be you.

Umm... Uh... Like... [deep breath]... You Know.

If you have come to this chapter expecting me to suggest that you take that piece you've recorded and have an AI go through it to remove every instance of "Um", or "Uh", take out your breath noises and mouth clicks, you will be disappointed.

In fact, some self-appointed gurus might even be enraged, and give the book a terrible review on Amazon for this chapter alone.

Just as we discussed leveraging those things about your voice that make you sound like you and avoiding the introduction of fakery, the same idea applies here.

Real people say, "Um".

In fact, there is a significant amount of research out there that suggests gifted communicators, and people communicating complex ideas, might even use "Uh" or similar words even more than others.

Rather than thinking of, "Um" as an irritant, think of it as a placeholder. Skilled communicators will often use words like, "Um" as a subtle signal that something else is coming, that perhaps isn't fully baked yet. Sometimes, pauses are there to heighten tension or highlight something important. Other times, it's to let you know that the speaker isn't yet finished the thought they're in the middle of. Maybe it's even there so that you can subconsciously fill in the space yourself; for example, if someone comes to you and asks if you'd like to be shoved feet-first into a wood chipper, you could look at them and say, "Umm…", and maybe even pause for a good six or seven seconds before saying the word that everyone knows would come next.

…at least, I hope everyone knows.

The point is that filler words, breath sounds, mouth clicks and such are all part of natural human speech. Often, those elements are there by design, and they are tools we all use. In fact, the hill I'm going to die on here is that because filler words, breath noises and mouth clicks are *so* common as parts of natural human speech, any process (mechanical or otherwise) that seeks to eliminate and eradicate them turns that speech into something that sounds *unnatural*.

As we discussed in Chapter 2, unnatural is distracting, and gets in the way of effective communication.

Am I suggesting that you should leave *every* "Um…" in there? No. Definitely not. If you're in the middle of a thought, and the 20 seconds it's taking you to come up with *exactly* the right word to use is peppered with nothing but "Uh… um…", then I might start looking around to see if that wood chipper is still available. But as with all things, there's a balance to be struck, and generally it's a process of experimentation.

If you leave them all in there, it could be root canal.

If you take them all out, then you might as well hand a transcript of what you want to say over to a text-to-speech app and have *that* thing do your voice work for you.

One of the reasons human voice actors will always be able to find work is because an AI will never be able to fully express emotion and the drama of everyday speech.

So do humanity a favor. Leave some of the “Ums” in once in a while. The survival of our species might count on it.

Scripts, and When to Use Them

As of this writing, we're a few weeks removed from the next Presidential election in the United States, and as a student of communication (both verbal and non-verbal), it's a fascinating time for me.

Media coverage is dominated by the latest thing this-or-that candidate said when they veered off-script, or how they haven't done many media interviews because they can't be trusted unless they have talking points to lean on, or how the only reason they've gotten as far as they have is because they have great speechwriters.

Political candidates might as well be contestants on *American Idol*, because on a show like that the audience only cares about whether you can hit the high note. They don't care about whether you know anything about music, whether you're able to communicate the emotion in a song, or any of the elements that traditionally help separate the wheat from the chaff in the world of music.

I'm sitting this morning in Canada, where the country is led by two very different versions of Prime Minister Justin Trudeau. There's Prime Minister Trudeau, who... speaks... very... deliberately... and... thoughtfully... to... the... point... of... being... robotic. And then there's Justin, who rolls up his sleeves, says "Um" a lot, gets emotional from time to time, and tells you what he really thinks. Sometimes, if you watch carefully, you can even see the wheels turning as he thinks to himself, “Do I *really* want to say this out loud?”

The reason for the difference is obvious: Sometimes he’s reading from a teleprompter, sometimes he’s not. And to date, his handlers haven’t found an effective “middle ground” for him.

To me, the middle ground for a true leader is obvious: Bullet points. While I understand that the subjects and ideas in a speech by a world leader might be of more consequence than on tomorrow’s installment of the “Britches and the Knickerknots” show on BoopdeyBoop Radio, one would hope that a world leader would occasionally be confident enough - and informed enough - about their own policies and ideas to be able to expound upon them extemporaneously, without fear of consequence. But I also recognize that from time to time, you’ll need cues to remember specific details.

As an example of this, I worked with a political candidate once who had been accused of being somewhat wooden in their delivery. We focused on eliminating much of the content from his teleprompter and his written notes, and instead focused on things that would trigger the ideas he was passionate about. Rather than an exhausting couple of paragraphs about the minutiae of policy, we simply had “School lunches - Catherine - Springfield.” Once he saw those words, he was reminded of an encounter he had with a specific constituent in a specific town who asked him about a specific subject. And we were confident enough that he was passionate enough to avoid blurting out something that would torpedo his chances at re-election.

Few things can damage the perception of the authenticity of a candidate more than having them lose their place in the teleprompter - or worse, having the teleprompter crash completely - and left with nothing to say.

One of the first habits I try to break for my coaching clients, whether on a podcast, a radio show or even a TV talk show - is to eliminate their dependence on scripts.

If you're an anchor reading a news story, then obviously the prompter is critical so you can relay the material facts of the story with 100% accuracy. But even then, I'll tell you the story of Brian Bourke.

Brian was the News Director for a radio station in the Toronto area where we worked together on a morning show in the 1990s.

Vacation and scheduling issues led to our first day on the air together also being the day we met. And so my first experience with Brian was watching him through the glass as he read the 5am news. That experience was... to say the least... unsettling.

Brian started the newscast looking straight at me. No, not looking into a camera, because this was radio. He was looking me right in the eye as the newscast started. And for the entire duration of the 4-minute newscast, he never took his eyes off me. Never looked at his script, never even glanced at the clock until about ten seconds before the commercial break at the end of the newscast.

He came out of the news booth, we shook hands and I said, "You never took your eyes off me. Will that be an everyday thing?" Brian said, "I hope not. The computer with my script on it, crashed at the exact moment you started the intro theme music for the newscast."

He had no script.

How was he able to do it? Brian's method for getting through his newscast off-the-cuff was the exact same method I've espoused for years: There absolutely was a script, but Brian wrote it himself, using the same language that he would use for everyday speech. So there were no curve balls, nothing tricky he had to remember, nothing disingenuous that would require effort to recall.

I say the same thing to countless coaching clients: Get comfortable with the idea that you are worth listening to, and that you don't need words on a page in order for you to have something interesting to say. Or, as I put it to a client who had recently gotten married:

You weren't reading from a teleprompter on the night you met your husband. (Well, at least I *hope* not, or that would have been awkward.) So you can apparently express yourself in a way that some people find interesting. And at least one person found it **really** interesting. Why do you think it's different when it comes to your show?

Think about your most passionate real-life conversations that took place without a single microphone over the course of a lifetime. Did you have notes in front of you? No. You didn't need them, because you had a subject you were interested in, something you knew about, and the comfort and confidence to communicate your ideas.

Isn't that what your show is supposed to be?

There are two ways I recommend to tackle this, and I still use both of them virtually every time I sit down in front of a microphone.

Method One: Write a Script in Your Own Voice

I have a podcast that is meant to sound like it is basically off-the-cuff, riffing on a particular subject that is of interest to me. Usually, because this is a technique I like to use, the last line of the episode tends to relate somehow to the very first line. As a result, I script that show in order to avoid going down a rabbit hole of conversation that makes it difficult for me to get back to the initial point I was trying to make. However, that doesn't mean the show still isn't off-the-cuff riffing. That portion comes while I am writing the script. Every sentence of the script is written as if it were simply a transcript of what I would have said in a live conversation. Then, my only task is to capture the same energy in the recording session as I had when I wrote the original script.

The script for a non-fiction audiobook can work the same way. The audio version of this book is done that way, and the book is written in a style that is not unlike the way I speak every day. If you ever stumble upon the audiobook version of this text, hopefully my comfort with that style of writing comes through.

One of my favorite audiobooks is by comedian Paul Reiser - you probably remember him from the runaway hit TV series, *Mad About You*, or in his much more serious role in the Netflix series *Stranger Things*. His first book was called *Couplehood*, and because of the way Paul wrote the manuscript, the audiobook sounded like Paul Reiser doing stand-up comedy. Inflections, reactions, subtleties in his delivery were all captured the way they would have been in front of a live audience or in a real conversation.

I'll admit that it's probably easier for Paul Reiser to write down his stand-up routine in text form, because he's used to delivering the material. It's similarly easy for me to write in a more conversational style because I spent forty years talking into microphones, so I know my speech patterns, turns of phrase and the places where I would pause or add emphasis.

It might not be quite as easy for you to do that.

...yet.

(***Spoiler Alert***: *The longer you wait to get started, the longer the skill will take to master.)*

Method Two: Bullet Points

If the material you're delivering is designed to be conversational, and it's a subject in which you have a solid base of foundational knowledge, then perhaps bullet points would be your best option.

(***Sidebar***: *I wrote that paragraph to be deliberately wordy, because I probably would never use "in which" in a regular conversation, nor would I use "perhaps". My guess is that it will show through that way for people listening to the audiobook version of this text. That's an example of what writing in your speaking voice can do for you.)*

Bullet points allow you to riff on whatever it is you're talking about in a manner that will come across to your audience as completely natural, because the conversation part *is* completely natural. All the bullet points do is serve as guardrails to keep you from going too far off-course, or to remind you of important points you wanted to be sure to include.

How much detail goes into the bullet points depends largely on the format of what you're doing, and the level of detail required in what you want to say. If you're reading them from a teleprompter, you're probably going to want to lay out a sequential list of points in the order you want to cover them.

For example, if I were going to take the text of this book and deliver it as a keynote, I would probably have a prompter, a cue card, or several sheets of paper taped to the floor of the stage, that simply contained the chapter titles from the book. That would be enough to trigger the ideas I wanted to get across, and because most of the ideas expressed here are concepts I have espoused for decades, I don't really need a lot of notes to cover the things I want to say.

However, if I needed to remember the part from Chapter 2 where I mentioned that Sean Hannity has 16 million listeners, I might want to give the "16 million" part its own line in a list of bullet points.

If you're using a prompter on television, it's worth remembering that your screen only displays a limited amount of text, and either you or the operator in the control room is going to need to scroll around your list of bullets to find what you need to get to, so you might have limited flexibility in what you're trying to cover.

If you're sitting in a radio booth or in your home studio where there's no camera, you can simply load your bullet points into a Google Doc or whatever word processor you're using and read it straight from the screen. Some clients have told me they prefer a bulleted list that's on paper, so they can cross off items on the list with a Sharpie as they cover them.

Speaking of a Sharpie...

How to Become Your Own Coach

I've had people question the wisdom of giving out this nugget, because it has cost many a guru some potential paying clients. However, while it's true that a ton of folks might want to improve their next show, it's not necessarily true that everyone can afford a coach to work with them one-on-one.

(Let's talk about that when you get to the "Afterword" section at the end.)

I've always offered this "hack" as a way of making some version of coaching accessible to virtually anyone. And now, with speech-to-text technology, it's available for free (or almost free) to anyone with a computer.

The one promise I can make you is that 100% of the time, this process will work better if you do it exactly as I lay it out, with no shortcuts or workarounds.

The method is simple: Take the audio from your last show, and use whatever tool you need to get a detailed transcript of it. If you want to use the TTS tool in something like Microsoft Word, great. Otter.ai? Terrific. Hire a virtual assistant from the other side of the planet or from Fiverr to transcribe it manually for a few bucks? Cool.

Once you have that transcript, print it out on paper. No, don't look at it on a screen. Print it out on paper.

This part is important, and it relates directly to the next step.

Grab your transcript, and a Sharpie. Yes, a Sharpie. Don't use the "Backspace" key, or a highlighter color in your word processor. Paper and a Sharpie. These elements really are critical to the entire process, and I'm going to ask you to trust me when I say it will make a difference.

Now you're going to take your transcript and, word by word, you're going to use your Sharpie to cross out all the words that don't belong there.

The things you're going to cross out might simply be filler words (see Chapter 3), it might be repetitive phrases or redundant sentences, it might be spots where you and your co-host were talking over each other, or myriad other elements that, given the choice, would have been omitted from a script you were writing in advance.

The Sharpie and the paper are important elements for this procedure because your brain will process it differently if there is a tactile element to it. Something about the act of physically crossing out a line of text on a page causes your brain to treat it differently than it would selecting and highlighting it on a screen. You'll have to ask a neuroscientist to explain the specifics of it, but it really does work.

When you've gone through the entire show, you might have a bunch of pages with a ton of black ink on them, looking like a legal document with the sensitive parts redacted.

Great! Now comes the fun part.

Now, take the editing you just did and learn to do it *before* the things you crossed out come out of your mouth. It's a pre-emptive strike that will prevent you from having to edit later.

For example: If you cross out the word "Um" 47 times, then you will gradually learn to say the word "Um" a lot less frequently. As one student said to me, "Every time I caught myself saying 'Uh' on the air, I thought about having to take a Sharpie later and cross it out."

If there's one tool in this book I would recommend adopting above and beyond all others, it's this one. I've yet to meet a single person who speaks into a microphone who hasn't benefited from using this method of pre-editing.

Throw Away Your Crutches

One of the most valuable pieces of the Sharpie process is that it will help you to identify the things you lean on a little too heavily.

As an example - I spent over a decade as a "talking head" on a cable news network. The anchor would set up a news story, then come to me for my take on it. I noticed, after going through the Sharpie process with the archived footage of my appearances, that I started most answers by saying, "Look..." So the anchor would say something like, "Neil, do you think the voters will be swayed by something like this?" I'd respond with, "Look, debates tend to be the place people to go *reinforce* their decisions rather than *reevaluate* them." While the rest of the answer might have some value, the word "look" was completely superfluous. And it was a speech pattern that had crept in over time and taken root, to the point where most segments in a show would include me saying that word, then getting on with the rest of my answer.

It sounds like a small thing, but many of us have crutches we lean on that really only serve to dilute whatever it is we're talking about.

One person I worked with had a habit of using the word "alright" as almost a verbal representation of a comma. He'd say things like, "What we have to do, alright, is to take a look at the situation, alright, and come up with answers that really serve our customers... alright?"

Here's why these crutches matter: Your brain, in its attempts to streamline incoming data, tends to skim over the things it doesn't interpret as relevant. The more crutches are present in your communication, the more skimming your brain will do. However, if those crutch words are pervasive, much of the content *between* the crutch words will also be lost.

Some more examples of attention-killing crutch words, especially when they appear at the beginning of a sentence:

- Honestly
- Anyway
- You know
- Okay
- Literally
- Ultimately
- Well
- The thing is
- In the final analysis
- At the end of the day
- Of course

- After all

It goes without saying that there are countless others, and you can probably identify a number of them yourself. If they're sprinkled about judiciously, you have nothing to worry about. When they start to become a feature of everything you say, you risk sending your audience a signal that it's safe to tune out.

The whole point of editing is to maximize the impact of your content; think of it like the culinary process known as a *reduction*. You can concentrate and intensify the flavor of whatever you're cooking by simply letting it simmer and allowing excess water to evaporate. That metaphor works in another way, though, because you can think of those crutch words as things that are watering down your content or making it less flavorful.

Are You Talking To Me?

My very strong hunch is that when De Niro envisioned himself asking that question in the movie, *Taxi Driver*, he was not asking an imaginary radio host if he was their intended audience.

There are two critically important questions that should be asked by everyone who sits in front of a microphone to talk to others. These questions apply to everything from keynote addresses to podcasts to radio shows and beyond and for the sake of streamlining, we'll refer to these things as a "show".

1. What is this show *about*?
2. Who is this show *for*?

You need crystal-clear answers to both questions in order to move forward on a path toward success.

My hope is that the first one is easy, but I'm occasionally surprised by how many people haven't considered a bullet-proof answer for it. And let's be clear: There isn't really a *wrong* answer, simply an ill-advised one. The question applies to podcasts, sure, but when you consider it, it's also relevant for radio shows and even for a TV morning show.

So what's your show about?

My favorite answer to this when I actually had a morning show of my own (and this works for both radio and television), was that we were the group of friends you sit with at the local diner for breakfast every morning. We talk about the interesting things that have happened since yesterday's get-together, and there are cool tunes, too. That's an oversimplification, of course, but that was the vibe I was going for. We were the comfy place to hang out with friends and catch up on the world before you start your day.

The nature of a podcast means that you're likely dealing with a more specific topic; talking about what happened since yesterday is difficult to maintain with a piece of on-demand audio that can be downloaded six months from now.

So what's your podcast about?

Star Wars,you say? Hmm. Okay. Do you know what comes up when I Google the term "*Star Wars* podcast"? An article titled, " The 70 Best *Star Wars* Podcasts You Must Follow". Imagine if there were only 70! The truth is there are *hundreds* of them, if not thousands. That article purports to whittle it down to the 70 *best* offerings.

If you want to be one among the 70, have at it. That was the problem that ultimately led to the death of radio. Listeners started to realize that radio stations had spent so much time and effort on being just another one of the many choices, that there were equally compelling choices beyond the borders of their own towns, so they moved over to sources on the internet. A friend pointed out to me once that there were nine stations in our city who were all "fighting over the same Kelly Clarkson record". They all ran similar ad campaigns on social media and even on transit buses, with photos of Michael Buble, Kelly Clarkson and Beyonce. That's a lot of wasted money to tell me that you're exactly like eight other stations in town.

If you're less likely to stand out, you're less likely to be missed. So what can you add to your description for your *Star Wars* podcast that will make it stand out from the crowd?

Maybe it's helpful, as you're trying to zero in on a more specific description of what your show is about, to determine who your show is *for*. That also involves having the courage to decide who it *isn't* for, and to get comfortable with that.

Think of it this way:

You have a friend who's a vegetarian. Not a vegan, but a vegetarian. The two of you go to Pizza Hut. The server comes over and says, "the special tonight is a large Meat Lover's pizza for $9.99." Your friend says, "Oh, but I'm a vegetarian."

In that moment, the server has two choices: First choice, a brief yet awkward silence followed by a tortured, heartfelt apology, then a retreat to find the manager who will promise that going forward, to avoid offending any other vegetarians, the restaurant will stop serving the Meat Lover's pizza.

The second choice has the server immediately look at your friend and say, "That's okay, that pizza's not *for* you." And thankfully, because it's Pizza Hut, the server can follow up with, “But we *do* have a ton of other options that might work for you, including the Veggie Lover’s pizza.” And although it has nothing to do with the point of this discussion, if that server is really good at their job they could also throw in, “I’ve tried that one myself and it’s one of my favorites.”

But the most important part is making peace with the idea that if you’re a vegetarian, the Meat Lover’s pizza is not for you. And that’s okay. It’s not up to Pizza Hut to change the Meat Lover’s pizza. It’s up to the person who walked into the restaurant to either find something on the menu they *do* like, or go somewhere else. Because if Pizza Hut did an effective job at figuring out their niche, they’re okay with the idea that not everyone is going to love everything on their menu.

Figuring out a niche is a big deal, no matter what you’re getting into. I’ve been involved in an unsettling number of conversations on social media lately where someone will jump into a discussion group for entrepreneurs and ask a question like, “I’ve just taken over a 3,000 square-foot space downtown that I got for an amazing deal. What business should I put in there?” I’m not making that one up. That question was *actually* asked.

Niches are a big deal in the podcast space right now; guru after guru seems to be hanging out their shingle based on their ability to help new podcasters “niche down”, and for whatever reason, the idea seems to meet with some resistance.

Maybe podcasters are just used to being the underdogs. Or being thought of as "less than". Or whatever it is that leads us to feel the need to endlessly tweak, mess with and otherwise "fix" our shows. Or maybe it's that because from a content perspective, podcasting has virtually *no* barriers to entry, and so we didn't invest enough time doing the market research that is such a critical piece of launching virtually *any* other venture that you're hoping to see succeed.

Let's zoom in on the podcasting element of this for a second, although it's very easy to apply these same principles to any pursuit or business, from choosing a sport to opening a car repair shop.

I asked one podcaster whether they had defined their target audience, and they proudly answered that they'd gotten *very* specific. They'd painstakingly arrived at the conclusion that their audience was 35 year-old women.

...and that was it.

I'm going to introduce you to two fictitious women to help illustrate why that's grossly insufficient, Mary and Brighton. Both women are 35, and this podcaster was going to do a show that would appeal to both of them.

Let's examine that for a beat. Mary lives in Cookeville, Tennessee. Brighton lives in San Francisco. Just on that basis alone, you already start to get the idea that while those two 35 year-old women will have *some* things in common, there will probably be exponentially more things they *don't* have in common at all.

So picture the Venn diagram for Mary and Brighton. And picture that tiny little oval in the middle where the two circles overlap. And compare that to the massive amounts of circle that don't. If this podcaster is truly going to only drill down as far as doing a show for 35 year-old women, they're aiming for the tiny little spot where the circles intersect. To avoid alienating either one of them, they're going to stay away from anyplace where there's *no* overlap. The podcast that will come out as a result will be almost entirely superficial and won't make any attempts to connect on any *real* level with either woman. As a result it won't connect with either of them, and will become completely disposable. (Which is, again, what happened to terrestrial radio.) The host, who is working their ass off to stay in that tiny little area of overlap, will wonder why they never get any engagement, why their download numbers plateau, and why the show has become less fun to do. about sixteen or seventeen episodes in, they'll quit and either start a new podcast, or stop podcasting altogether.

It's the same for the car repair place. You want to open a garage, huh? Great. Did you know that in Mary's hometown of Cookeville, Tennessee, there are already at least twenty other garages? Everything from Midas and Firestone to Big Bob's over on West Broad. So if you're going to open a garage there, you're probably looking at *maybe* grabbing 4 or 5 percent of the local car repair market.

But what if you niche down?

What if instead of opening another garage, you open a garage for high-end cars? Maybe your garage only services *Italian* cars – so Fiat, Maserati, Lamborghini, Alfa Romeo and so on. Now, I'm not saying a place like that would catch on in Cookeville, but suddenly, instead of just being another one among the twenty, you can focus on being the ONE that gets the call when the Cizeta hits the fan. And by virtue of being *the one*, you can also charge more than the guys at Midas, because you offer a super-specialized service.

What if that podcaster niches down, and instead of 35 year-old women, they target 35 year-old women who are married to men that are addicted to *Star Wars*? And let's be honest, at that point you're probably done, because those streets might just be paved with gold – especially if you ditch the 35 year-old thing altogether and push those boundaries out to include, say, women 35 and up. "*On next week's show, we'll talk to a woman whose fiancé showed up at their wedding dressed as Chewbacca.*" The possibilities are endless. You might also find you're getting a higher than average rate from advertisers, because you've got a well-defined audience that isn't likely being duplicated by any other show.

So now you have a better idea of the audience you're trying to talk to, and what makes you unique. But in most cases, I recommend getting even more specific than that.

With that in mind, let's head out to the golf course.

Are You Talking To Me? (Pt 2)

Golfers have caddies for a couple of reasons. One PGA professional told me that while the caddy's most obvious job is to carry the clubs from one hole to the next, the best ones serve as sounding boards and as counsel to the player. As they walk up to the ball, the art of being a truly great caddy is on display. Knowing the wind speed and direction, knowing the difference in elevation between the spot where the ball is versus its intended target, knowing the exact distance from the ball to the hole, even the fact that the direction that the grass has been cut makes a difference in how far the ball will roll once it lands... all of these things help caddies stand out among the crowd.

When the caddy and the pro approach the ball, the caddy is usually the one agonizing over the exact distance to the hole, and the million other details that need to be considered. Based on those factors, the caddy then selects the exact club the pro needs for this shot, and offers advice on whether the swing needs a little more, or a little less than the baseline for that club, and where the pro should aim the swing to take the wind into account. There's an actual difference between which club you'll use, and how much effort you'll put in, for a 190-yard shot on a calm day versus a 189-yard shot with a slight breeze coming from the right. If the caddy gets those calculations exactly right, all the pro has to do is execute the swing, without worrying about all the details.

So it's great that the last chapter led you to define a more specific audience. Now, I'm going to give you a caddy. What if, every time you turned on the microphone, the work of determining who you're talking to had already been done, and all you had left to do was talk to them?

If you do this part right, you'll know exactly who they are. Whether you call them the avatar for your show, your ideal listener, your target audience, whatever you want – define with agonizing specificity who they are. Why? Because once you know who they are, the job of talking to them requires about one tenth of one percent of the work that's required if you're trying to talk to *everyone*.

At one radio station I worked with, we did a complete demographic and psychographic profile of our ideal listener. We even *named* her. (By the way, her name was Judy.) We knew Judy's job, how many kids she has, what those kids do, what kind of car she drives, we knew everything about her. Then we just did our shows for Judy. We even had a life-sized cardboard cutout of a model we'd hired that we thought embodied her. And everything the station did had to pass through the filter of, "Would Judy like this?" And as long as the answer was, "Yes", then we knew we were on course. Judy was our friend. Someone we enjoyed talking to, and someone we never wanted to let down.

AI photo generating tools are now so pervasive and so inexpensive that in a few minutes, you'll have a photo of your own Judy that you can put somewhere within your field of vision, and you can just talk to Judy (or Mary or Brighton or whoever else) as if they were right there in front of you.

I have a friend who does stand-up comedy and tells me that every night, he envisions his brother being in the crowd. At first, he did it so he'd stop obsessing over whether or not the audience *liked* him. If he did the show for his brother, he's got an audience he's comfortable talking to, who likes him, and who thinks he's funny. And it was much easier to focus on making his brother laugh than to get laughs from a bunch of random strangers.

Your alternative is that you can keep trying to talk to everyone. My experience with countless broadcasters and podcasters tells me that ends up translating into *genuinely* making *connections* with *no one*. Connecting with no one means never having *fans*. You just get casual listeners who might not even notice - never mind miss you - when you're gone.

And if you really want to make a genuine connection, it goes even further.

Are You Talking To Me? (Pt 3)

For podcasters and radio DJs alike, I think the gold lies in talking to *one* person. Yes, there might be three hundred thousand people listening right now, but your focus should be on talking only to *one* of them.

For most media, we're told that connection is key. "Gotta connect with your audience," they say – me included. But it's possible that you're subconsciously torpedoing that connection with some of the first words out of your mouth. The good news? It's very easy to correct. It might just involve breaking some habits that aren't serving you.

You've probably done it. I know I have. And many of the people we might look up to as content creators do it. If I wanted to put a happy spin on it, I'd say we get so wrapped up in thinking about the audience and who's watching or listening, that we forget *how* they watch or listen.

Truth is, though, that it's probably something we're doing out of laziness, out of habit, or – as was the case recently with one of my coaching clients – nobody ever pointed it out to us before. I've had pushback on what I'm about to describe to you, but this will be one of those times I'll just ask you to trust me. At the end of this chapter I'll put a bow on the idea for you that will hopefully forever cement it in your psyche. When you implement it, your audience will notice a difference, but it will be one of those little intangibles that they can't readily identify.

If we're talking about *normal consumer behavior*, we're told that people who are actively listening to spoken word audio – whether that's radio, podcasts or audiobooks – are usually listening alone. It makes sense, when you think about it, because when's the last time you grabbed the left AirPod, gave a friend the right AirPod, and proceeded to listen to nine hours of an audiobook together? And when I say "actively listening", I mean actually *listening* to content instead of *hearing* it. There's a difference. If you're rockin' out to "Don't Stop Believin'" by Journey with your friends in the car and you turn down the volume when the DJ comes on, you're not listening to the spoken word part anymore. You might *hear* it, but you're no longer paying attention.

Some forms of spoken-word content are *created* in an environment where people are watching or listening together. Most TV talk shows, for example, are done in front of a live studio audience. So David Letterman looked out from the stage and sure, he saw some cameras, but he also saw a couple of hundred people thirty feet away, looking back at him. When Jimmy Kimmel tells a joke, he hears them laugh. When Ellen starts one of her dance routines, the crowd gets into it, too, and if you're in the studio audience, the energy is electric. And the cameras very consciously show you the studio audience, or let you hear them laughing and applauding, or both.

That's not by accident; they are reminding you that you are a member of a large audience.

So if you grew up on a steady diet of Johnny Carson and Letterman like I did, you got used to seeing the host of a show say things like, "Alright, folks, here's who's on the show tonight." Or hearing Stephen Colbert refer to the audience as "My friends". And virtually everyone, from the Don Pardo announcer types on *Saturday Night Live* to carnival barkers often address a crowd by calling them "ladies and gentlemen". (Well... except at Disney.)

Now, for Letterman, calling the audience "folks" makes sense because that's what he sees. But when you're doing your radio show or your podcast, how many people do you see in the audience? Right. Zero. When you're writing the script for your radio commercial, how many audience members are looking back at you? Exactly none.

So who are *we* talking to when we say, "folks"? If we open our show by saying, "Hi guys" – *what* guys? I can't tell you the number of times I've heard someone open a show by saying, "Hey, everybody."

Let's remember... whether it's a podcast, the morning show on my favorite station or a radio commercial, what we're trying to build is a *connection.* A connection who will hopefully feel *so* connected to us that, sure, they're entertained and they want to hear more from us, but a connection that's strong enough to earn a *recommendation* to someone *else* they're connected to.

But if you're referring to "everybody", and I'm in the car by myself, you've just reminded me that you're not really talking to *me*. I'm incidental. My friend Dave Jackson from *The School Of Podcasting* talks about this in terms of those YouTube videos where the creator reminds you to "hit the bell and click 'subscribe'"... except that if I've already hit the bell and clicked 'subscribe', you just reminded me that this is a recording, you're not really sharing something with me, you were just talking into a camera and I happened to digitally eavesdrop.

If you believe I'm nit-picking with this notion, think of it this way. You and I are friends in real life who haven't hung out since the 45 minutes we spent together last week. I see you walking down the street - alone - and I come up to you. I shake your hand and say, "Hey, everybody, what's up?"

Are you seriously going to tell me there would be *no* disconnect for you in that moment?

And if the two of us kept having a conversation and I kept addressing you as "folks", and a couple of times I even called you "ladies and gentlemen", are you *honestly* not going to wonder what the f@#% is wrong with me?

But if I invite you into my car or my AirPods for 45 minutes, the connection is arguably even more intimate than a walk down the street.

This is exactly what I mean when I say that we tend to think about this connection from *our* side, instead of considering the perspective of the audience. And the audience has the only perspective that matters. If you have my attention, don't alienate me. Not if you're really looking for connection, or engagement, or whatever it is you want from me.

I Woke Up In A Soho Doorway

Now that you have a rock-solid description of what your show is about, and you've defined the exact one person you're talking to, there's another piece of this puzzle we've yet to establish.

Who are you?

I remember waking up one morning in a city where I had arrived the night before to do a keynote at a conference. I turned on the radio to hear one of the hosts having what could have been a very bad day.

It turned out, based on what I was able to piece together mid-show when I joined (more on that later), that he was embroiled in a rather high-profile divorce. And since yesterday's show ended, his wife had gone public with her thoughts on why she should win their ongoing custody battle, and a local media outlet had decided to run the story.

He was understandably upset, and actually apologized to the audience for being a little off his game that day.

Awkward, right?

Nope.

What happened instead was pure magic. Phone call after phone call - which his co-host insisted they should take live on the air - from listeners who were huge fans of the show, talking about what a great guy the host was, how they'd met him at this or that event and how he'd been so kind to them and generous with his time, and I remember clear as a bell a woman who called and said she'd seen him a couple of weeks earlier with his kids at a baseball game, and how she remembered thinking to herself what a wonderful, patient, attentive Dad he was - she even said that when he was ready for his next relationship, he should give her a call.

What I was listening to was a broadcaster who had done a spectacularly good job of establishing his character. In his case, his character happened to be *him*, but that's not always the case. Whether the person you portray on your show is simply an extension of yourself, or some fictitious character you have created, what's important is that just as you have drawn a very specific picture of your "Judy", your audience has a clear picture of you.

(Side note: if you put enough work into it, it is possible to make a character who is fictitious, yet so convincing that the audience forgets that they are watching a character. Comedian Andrew Dice Clay, for example, doesn't exist. He is a character portrayed in an ultra-convincing fashion by actor Andrew Silverstein.)

Again, we're talking about the difference between having an audience versus having fans. If you don't want fans, don't worry about this step. You'll just be that random person with another *Star Wars* show.

By defining who you are, you give your fans the extra level of comfort that comes from knowing what to expect in a given situation.

I had a client argue this point with me, saying that one of the things that made Robin Williams such a superstar is that you never knew what to expect, even from one second to the next. Except they were making my point *for* me, and even said it in their own wording... you "never" knew. As a result, you *always* knew that Robin Williams was going to do something unpredictable, and that was part of the joy of watching him, was the anticipation of whatever craziness was *inevitably* about to erupt. If there were ever a night when Robin Williams walked out on a stage and just did straight stand-up, the audience would have left disappointed, wondering where the trademark antics had gone.

But if you're getting together with someone for ten minutes a day, or 45 minutes a week or whatever other time you take up in their lives, there should be a level of comfort there.

If you went to a restaurant once a week and always had the same entree - maybe you love the way the chef grills your steak - you have an expectation of what's going to show up when the plate reaches the table. McDonalds has built a global business on the idea that a Big Mac should taste the same in Paris as it does in Peoria.

The friends you hang out with, the people you work with, the characters on the TV shows you watch...

they are all, to a degree, predictable. And that's true even if the most predictable thing about them is their unpredictability. Even then, though, we're brought back to the Robin Williams example. If your calling card is that you're "a wild and crazy guy" like Steve Martin was in the 1970s and 80s, then you'd better be wild and crazy every time you walk out on stage.

If you've made it clear on your *Star Wars* podcast that you *hate* everything about *Star Trek*, and then the YouTube version of your next episode features you wearing a t-shirt with Mr. Spock on it saying, "Live Long and Prosper", your fans are going to want to know what's going on. If no one asks, maybe it's because there are no fans. Just casual viewers and listeners who find you disposable, as they work their way to the next show on the list of the 70 Best *Star Wars* Podcasts.

If your friend with the long blonde hair suddenly shows up one night with a Marine-style buzz cut that's been dyed orange, you're going to want to know why, or at least comment on it.

Your audience should have just as clear a picture of you. If not, you're not bringing enough of yourself to the show. And *you* are what makes your show truly unique. *Star Wars* is not unique. A podcast about *Star Wars* is not unique. The unique part is your take on it. What can *you* say about it that isn't being said on every other show in that list of 70? That depends on what happens to the topic after it has passed through "The You Filter".

Three more perfect examples of this, and then I think we'll let the horse rest...

1. There was a time - though it may be difficult to imagine now - when significant events happened in pop culture or in the news, that people couldn't wait to see how it would be treated on *Saturday Night Live*, because it was expected that certain items would be featured. The clearest memory I have of this mindset was during the OJ Simpson murder trial, when people would refer to Norm MacDonald's *Weekend Update* segment when something big happened in the trial by saying, "I can't wait to hear what Norm says about this."

2. When Howard Stern had a show on terrestrial radio, his listeners would routinely sit through seven-minute sets of commercials, because they didn't want to miss whatever Howard was going to say when he came back. Howard's audience had a very clear expectation of the kinds of things he was going to say, and Howard rarely strayed from what his audience was waiting for.

3. Rush Limbaugh had the biggest radio talk show in history. His wasn't the only political talk show on the air, but there are many who will tell you that Republican voters in the United States would take their cues and form their opinions from what Rush had to say

> about current events. They knew what to expect from him, and they were comfortable enough with his well-established history of opinions to be sure that they would probably agree with whatever he was about to say. The same was true of his opponents. All you had to hear was that Rush Limbaugh had weighed in on a particular topic, and one side or the other would already know whether they agreed or not simply by hearing that it was Rush's opinion.

Hosts with clearly-defined characters have fans. One fan beats ten listeners every day of the week.

The Sheldon Cooper Effect

This chapter was initially going to be called "The Smartest Kid in the Room", but then I realized there's a television character who kind of embodies all the points I'm going to try to make here.

Dr. Sheldon Cooper is one of the main characters on the TV show *Big Bang Theory*. Sheldon has an IQ of 187 (anything over 130 is considered "Very Superior"). Sheldon is always the smartest kid in the room during virtually every conversation, and has no problem letting you know about it.

As a result, most "normal" people find Sheldon quite annoying and difficult to endure.

Don't be like Sheldon.

I worked with an announcer once who possessed a virtually encyclopedic knowledge of music from the Rat Pack era. Sinatra, Martin, Armstrong, Fitzgerald... all of the legends of big band and jazz music were his jams, and he loved to talk about them. His love for the music was inspiring.

Sometimes, however, his love for even the tiniest elements of the music are on display when he's seeking to correct something someone else has said, and the line gets blurred between "interesting fact" and "annoying minutiae".

One day, on the air, he decided to "school me" on the correct pronunciation of an artist's name. I had just finished playing “What A Wonderful World” in honor of the birth of legendary trumpeter and singer Louis Armstrong. Now, if you’re like most people I know, you just read the artist’s first name and the voice in your head said “Louie”. My Sheldon-esque friend, who was part of the show that morning, jumped in to let me know that “Louie” was actually incorrect, and that Armstrong himself preferred that people pronounce it like “Lewis”.

I myself have done the same thing. It’s a minor irritant for me when people are talking about measurements in the Metric system, and they talk about distances being in (forgive my attempt to write it phonetically) and say the word “kilometers” by pronouncing it “kill - AW - mit -urz”, instead of the correct version, “KILL - oh - meet - urz”. Off the cuff one day, I started going into detail about all the evidence I had to support my point, until I realized that I had turned into Sheldon Cooper.

People don’t enjoy being corrected. They especially loathe being corrected over meaningless things.

But there I was, shaking my fist toward the sky like the Lieutenant Dan character at the top of the mast in *Forrest Gump*, angrily challenging the sky and yelling, “YOU CALL THIS A STORM? IT’S TIME FOR A SHOWDOWN!” I blamed Mr. Sulu on *Star Trek*, I went into detail about how it’s the only word in the entire Metric system where we change the emphasis, and had become the exact thing I loathed.

There's a difference between pointing out something genuinely interesting, and nit-picking.

If someone tells you that "less than 500 people showed up" and you reply by saying, "you mean 'fewer' than 500 people showed up", you're guilty as charged.

If someone is telling a story, and they mention they were writing something in pencil and they broke the lead, and you interrupt the story to say that pencils actually don't contain lead and never have, it's actually a combination of clay and graphite, you're guilty as charged.

I think of these little sidebar nuggets almost like the signs on the side of the highway to let you know there's a truck stop ahead: One of the main things they emphasize is, "Easy On, Easy Off". They mean that taking the time to stop there won't pull you very far off the highway, and won't add a ton of time to your trip.

If the thing you're adding to the conversation doesn't *derail* the conversation, then you're probably safe. But if the person you've decided to interrupt has to get back to the main story by saying, "Anyway…", then you're suffering from The Sheldon Cooper Effect.

One further favorite example comes from the music world, in the form of singer / guitarist Randy Bachman, the guy you hear on the song "Takin' Care Of Business". Randy's last name is actually pronounced “BACK - mun”, but people see the letters “Bach” and they think of the composer, so they mispronounce Randy’s name as “BOCK - mun”. Randy himself says that he realized *everyone* was pronouncing it wrong, and constantly correcting them was becoming exhausting, so after a while he just stopped.

Sometimes this means taking that microsecond it takes for a thought to leave your brain and head toward your mouth, and evaluate whether it is actually contributing to the conversation that’s in progress, or throwing up a roadblock.

Always, always, always choose to contribute. Nobody likes running into roadblocks.

Your Equipment: Style vs Substance

The first time I spoke into a microphone in front of an audience, it was 1974. I was in third grade, and as part of a homework assignment I was giving a speech in front of our whole school on a particular dialect of British English that's specific to the Northeast of England, where the people are known as Geordies. I did about eight minutes of what essentially was stand-up comedy, translating Geordie phrases into plain English. I was hooked by the experience. Less than ten years later I was working as a DJ on the radio, and by 1985 I was doing *actual* stand-up.

So I've been speaking into microphones, and scripting, recording, mixing and editing *other* people who speak into microphones, for more than fifty years. And the bottom line is this: I know, beyond anyone's reasonable ability to debate, what a good microphone sounds like, and what a bad microphone sounds like. I'm not quite at the level of expertise possessed by my old friend Bob Doidge – who once had to FedEx a Neumann U47 to Ireland because Bono insisted on using that specific microphone to record the vocals for *The Unforgettable Fire* in a mossy, mildewy old castle – but I know a good mic from a bad one.

There's a podcast I do where the most popular episode ever released was recorded using a twenty-dollar microphone.

I didn't get it at a garage sale, or inherit it from a long-deceased relative. Bought it brand new for twenty bucks. Another element that was offensive to the podcasting illuminati was that I bought it off Amazon. And the death blow to my future as a Podcasting Cool Kids Club member? It was a lapel mic.

What I was beginning to understand, much to my disappointment, was that there are some in the podcast space that have set forth kind of a nebulous list of "minimum requirements" for podcast production – kind of the same way your computer has minimum requirements to run a particular piece of software. The implication is that anything less than these minimums will result in a show that's unlistenable. What that has resulted in, is the deliberate construction of false barriers to entry. You have to spend a certain amount on your microphone, they'll say. And you need to spend money on software to produce your podcast, or have a certain amount of technological prowess to allow you to navigate the feature sets of the freebies. And heaven forbid you should use one of those free podcast hosting services. How gauche. Next you'll be telling the elitists that you don't plan on spending hundreds of dollars on acoustic foam for your dedicated recording space. The horrors.

As a person who's been in broadcasting at a very high level since the early 1980s, here's what I will tell you with indisputable certainty: If you've booked an interview with Ryan Reynolds, Mick Jagger or even the ridiculously overexposed Elon Musk – and I mean “overexposed” in about three different senses of the word – and they’re doing the interview through a drive-thru speaker, there will be tons of people who will listen. And I’ll additionally promise you this: At least 90% of the people who will be critical of the audio quality, will be people in the industry.

Rolling Stones fans want to hear what Mick Jagger has to say. And the only thing they care about is that Mick sounds good enough that they can easily understand what he’s saying – in fact, they don’t even care about THAT. Because they’re not thinking about it. Not thinking about it at all, unless his audio is so garbled and distorted that you can’t understand him. That’s the only time audio quality even *occurs* to them. They don’t care if his audio is at 384k or 32k. As long as they can hear it. They won’t write a scathing review about how you obviously didn’t use the low-end rolloff switch on your RE-20. It’s like most anything else – you don’t notice something until it is obviously wrong. You don’t notice the function of your left knee, for example, until your left knee hurts. You don’t think about the marvels of your charger cable until the cable stops working properly. You only think about the functionality of your can opener when it’s not opening cans anymore.

If the concept is anathema to you, that listeners don’t tend to think at all about audio quality unless it sucks, that’s okay. It happens to everybody at one point or another. To tons of people I know who are legends in their respective media, whether that’s podcasting, TV, movies, radio, whatever – it happens multiple times. Regularly, even. In radio, we used to describe it as having to remember how to "listen like a listener". You spend long enough as a broadcaster, you forget how to listen and evaluate things the way the average listener would. As further examples, you'll get tired of your intro theme, or the jingle in your commercials, in about a tenth of the time it'll take before the audience will. Because they don't hear it the same way you do. You're coming at it from different places.

It reminds me of the first time I saw the movie *The Return Of The Jedi*. I saw it in a theater with my friend Rob Petrovicz, who was seeing it – without a word of hyperbole – for something like the 44th time. That's not to be critical of Rob in any way, he went on to become a massive deal in science fiction television; but for me that day, it meant that in the middle of one of the climactic battle scenes Rob leaned over and said, "Look! You can see the reflection of the camera crew in C3PO's head!"

SHUT UP, ROB. I'M TRYING TO WATCH A MOVIE.

But we were there for different reasons. I was there to watch the story unfold. Rob was there to nitpick the technical details because the technical details were his passion. A passion that turned into an award-winning career. To him, the story was secondary, because the passion was in the behind-the-scenes part of telling it.

The dirty little secret that the gurus won't admit to is this: Your ***fans*** don't love your audio quality. They love your ***content***. If you don't have fans, or don't know how to convert listeners into fans, or don't know how to do the kind of content that ***gets*** you fans, there's no microphone in the world that can save you. (Not even Bob Doidge's U47, which I think he's still cleaning the moss out of.) Something like 150 million people a week still listen to talk radio in the United States. And on talk radio, about half the airtime is taken up by people who are on the ***phone***. No one cares about the audio quality of the people on the phone because the talk radio audience isn't there for audio quality. They're there for the ***content***.

However, my experience has been that when you have reached the peak of your ability to improve the quality of the content, your attention turns to improving the quality of the sound.

The self-appointed gatekeepers seem to want you to forget that in the majority of cases, your audio is being delivered after having been converted from actual *audio* to a low-resolution digital file, which is then being broadcast across a Bluetooth radio signal into ear buds with a limited frequency response, likely in a place where the listener is also dealing with a ton of ambient noise. Just how good are you demanding this recording should be?

The truth is, much to the chagrin of the Podcasting Cool Kids Club, that you can do a show with audio quality that is perfectly acceptable, with a twenty-dollar lapel microphone. And I can back up that assertion with nearly fifty years of experience with microphones that cost everywhere from eighteen dollars to eighteen hundred dollars. And if you still need what could be described as a pun-worthy "mic drop moment" in this chapter, consider this: Virtually every anchor on every television newscast, and every host on late night television, uses a lapel mic. And no one I'm aware of has ever complained about the quality of their audio.

Pretending that you need something better, and erecting false barriers to entry, is preventing us from hearing from potentially powerful voices in already marginalized communities.

So before you run to your powerful keyboard and start a Twitter movement in support of my lifetime ban from the Podcasting Cool Kids Club, maybe stop for a second and examine whether your perspective is the result of your privilege.

How to Do a Great Interview

A lot of the podcasters and broadcasters I work with hit a roadblock when it comes to doing interviews. They can have solo shows, team shows and for whatever reason, the Q-and-A format of an interview just seems to throw them a curve ball that they can't hit.

So let me throw some ideas at you here that work 100% of the time for my coaching clients.

For starters, remember this: The most likely reason you are doing this interview in the first place is because your guest has something they want to promote, whether it's an event, a media property of their own, or even simply to distribute a point of view in the name of building their own awareness.

In other words: They *want* this conversation to go well.

And sorry if I burst your bubble about the whole, "something to promote" thing. You didn't seriously think that all those huge stars go on with Jimmy Kimmel just because they love his company, did you? I mean, I'm sure he's a lovely guy, but... come on...

So when you take into consideration that your guest wants the conversation to go well, remember this: An interview is simply a conversation that is so compelling, it's worth eavesdropping on. If you want it to be compelling, the best way to get there is by appealing to your guest's passions. And in most cases, their passion-de-jour is the thing they're there to promote. There are exceptions, but we'll get there in a minute.

To me, the first, best thing you can do - especially if your guest doesn't do many interviews - is to let them off the hook. Let them know that it's YOUR job to make the interview sound good. I would say to guests who didn't have much experience, "Listen... I'll worry about sounding like a professional announcer. YOU think about sounding like Mary who has the fundraiser at the hospital that she really cares about." Most of the time, that was enough to get them to take a deep breath and relax.

Now here is the thing that frustrates me about some interviews, but keep in mind that I've done somewhere around ten to twelve ***thousand*** interviews over the course of a career, and there's one thing that has always served me very well.

Sometimes, especially when you're booking a guest who's either inexperienced, or maybe a really big star, or maybe the spokesperson for the government or a major corporation, you'll be asked to provide the interview questions in advance.

My answer to this request has been the same for decades, and it's this:

I don't know what Question 2 will be, until I have heard the answer to Question 1.

My interviews aren't so much interviews as conversations, hopefully between people who sound like friends.

So think of the last time you were at a party, and you got introduced to someone new. Did you pull out a list of questions that you had prepared in advance? No. You asked what was hopefully an interesting first question, and the conversation carried on from there.

And you could make the argument that a conversation at a party is even ***harder*** than an interview, because in theory, the person you just met isn't using the conversation to promote their latest project.

So for me, with one notable exception, I really only plan the first question for any interview. Now... because I tend to only interview people I actually find interesting, I almost always have some "rescue questions" in the back of my head in case something starts to go sideways, but those questions are almost always born exclusively by my genuine interest in that person, or perhaps a shared passion that we have that I became aware of in my interview prep, but my plan really is just for that first question, and I try to make it something that will spark a thoughtful response that will help move the conversation forward.

The one notable exception is this: I have a podcast called *The Snooze Button*, and it's basically a show that chronicles my lifelong search for a good night's sleep, talking in every episode to neuroscientists, sleep researchers and even celebrities with sleep challenges built in to their day-to-day lives. Every guest on that show, even if they've been on the show six or seven times before in its five-year history, gets the same first question: "How did you sleep last night?" The answer to that question almost always inspires a follow-up, because the guest usually talks about the quality of their sleep AND what might have contributed to that quality, for better or for worse.

But if you're going to take that road less-traveled and only come up with the first question, recognize that the weight of a compelling conversation has shifted to you, and it's now your responsibility to listen incredibly carefully to the answer, and be able to quickly find the springboard to your next question in there somewhere.

One of the main reasons I hate coming up with questions in advance, and the reason I recommend against doing it with my coaching clients, is that it kind of handcuffs you and takes you out of the moment.

Let me give you an example of what I mean. Say you're interviewing the guitar player from that great new band from England, and they're talking about their new album.

You consult the list of questions you supplied to the record company, and the interview goes something like this:

YOU: “So tell me about the process of recording this new album.”

STAR: “Well, we wanted a sound that was really authentic, you know? So we went into the drummer’s basement and recorded the entire album naked.”

YOU: “I see. So tell me about your musical influences.”

Don’t laugh - I’ve actually heard interviews that went that way.

This is also one of the reasons I recommend to my clients on both radio shows and podcasts that they should put together five minutes of original comedy material and try it out at the open-mike night in their town. You learn things in those five minutes that are almost impossible to learn anywhere else, and it will go a long way toward teaching you how to deal with situations like that.

But I’ll tell you about two specific situations where my approach served me incredibly well.

It’s the spring of 2009, and I’m doing a morning show in a bedroom community near Washington DC. My guest that morning is the late, great Annie Wersching, who guest stars in the last two seasons of the TV series *24* as an FBI agent who becomes Jack Bauer’s girlfriend.

Her performances are so compelling in the show that everybody wants to talk to Annie Wersching. So she is doing the rounds on the big morning radio and TV shows, including mine. But as I'm doing my interview prep, I notice that every show she goes on, no matter how big or how small, is focused on the fact that as a child, Annie was a competitive Irish stepdancer. Several of the shows run footage of teenaged Annie in a competition. And this cycle repeated for dozens and dozens of interviews before mine.

So when I get Annie on the phone, before we went on the air, I said to her, "Just so you know... I promise there will not be a single question in this conversation about Irish stepdancing." She laughed and said, "Thank God." And then we rolled tape.

The interview went so well that Annie jumped on Twitter right after we hung up the phone, and tweeted about how refreshing it was to do an interview with someone who had actually done their homework, was actually interested and actually took the time to come up with original questions.

But to me, I was just genuinely interested in learning more about her, and talked to her the way I would talk to any person who I actually wanted to learn about. To this day, it remains one of my favorite interviews I've ever done. But guest stars on *24* had a habit of giving great interviews. Sean Astin still owes me dinner because he lost a bet we made on my show about whether his death scene in that show's 5th season was consistent with what allegedly killed him.

The second example is a little more interesting. It's September, 2014 and I'm doing a radio morning show in Toronto. Bryan Adams is coming to the studio to record an interview that will run on both radio and television, to promote his new album called *The Tracks Of My Years*. Now I'm a big Bryan Adams fan, and have been since his earliest recordings, so this will be a treat for me.

...except that this particular morning, we're catching Bryan toward the end of the media tour to promote the record, and frankly, he's tired. He didn't sleep well last night, he's exhausted from doing all the interviews, and he's bored with talking about the record.

So the cameras roll, and Bryan is sitting with me on a stage in front of a studio audience of around 100 people, with his arms folded across his chest. Already I can see that this is going to be interesting.

And with no offense to hockey players, the first few minutes of the interview were like the ones you see if you watch a hockey game, in between periods, where the players don't really have much to say. Bryan was giving me a lot of "Yes" and "No" answers, or answers that were 10 words or less. I mean, he was giving me nothing, and it was starting to get uncomfortable. So I called for a commercial break to give everyone a chance to reset, including me.

When we came back from the commercial, I relied on my pre-interview prep and reached back for those rescue questions. I figured that if he was tired of talking about the record, we'd talk about anything BUT the record. The company that owned the radio station also owned a magazine that Bryan routinely shot cover photos for. So we started talking about Bryan's passion for photography.

Suddenly, a light came on. The arms weren't folded across the chest anymore. He wasn't sitting back in his chair, he leaned forward with his elbows on his knees. And eventually, we went BACK to talking about the album with a Bryan Adams who was engaged and interested.

Now... what do you do if your guest isn't a person you find all that interesting, and you're not really jacked up about whatever it is they're promoting?

I guess the most obvious answer is... why are they on your show?

Wait - What Did I Miss?

As of this writing, I am ten episodes into a YouTube series I launched which essentially chronicles my attempts to teach myself how to play the piano.

It's something I've wanted to learn my whole life, but I've never taken lessons because more often than not they're cost-prohibitive, or because the teachers don't offer instruction that lines up with the way that I learn.

Yes, there are video series and lessons available online, but in the same way that this book can only guide you to a certain level, I need one-on-one coaching from someone who can actually teach *me* instead of the masses.

(Don't waste your time looking for the series... it's objectively awful. It's really only there because telling the audience that I'll record my practice sessions three times a week and post them online introduces some external pressure to actually make sure I practice.)

Sometime in the first couple of minutes of every episode, I stop to explain to the viewer that I'm getting on in years, and that I'm trying to teach myself about 20-25 songs to be able to realize a lifelong dream of being able to sing and play at a piano bar somewhere. I tell them I can read music, but only for one-note-at-a-time instruments like the trumpet, because you could play 10 notes at once on the piano (eleven if you use your foot like Jerry Lee

Lewis), and there's just far too much happening on a page of sheet music for me to be able to keep up. I add that while I'm a pretty competent singer, my brain doesn't have the ability to focus on what's happening with my left hand, what's happening with my right hand, what's happening with the foot pedal, to recall the lyrics to the song *and* to sing it, all at the same time. Something suffers and it ends up sounding awful.

I point all of this out in every episode. Often I'll also toss in the fact that I can hear random notes on a piano that will trigger memories of specific songs, owing to the decades I spent playing these songs on the radio.

I include all this detail because I have know way of knowing which episode will be the first one for the viewer. Maybe the 27th episode I release will be the first one they watch. And if I don't mention all the backstory, maybe they'll sit there thinking, "Why doesn't he just take lessons?" If that happens, they miss the point of the entire show and they won't become a fan.

I remember one of my stand-up friends had a bit that he would do the moment the first person in the audience got up to go to the restroom. When he did, he'd address the audience directly and say, "When they come back, do this for me - I'll say the word 'artichoke', and you laugh like it's the funniest thing you ever heard, okay?" And sure enough, the person would come back, he'd get to a sentence that included the word, "artichoke", the crowd would laugh and the comedy came from watching the victim react to being the only person in the room who wasn't in on the joke. In retrospect, it was kind of cruel by modern standards, but forty years ago, it was hilarious to watch them sit there completely oblivious and uncomfortable.

Trust me, that's not the feeling you want to give your audience.

We've discussed already in earlier chapters that making your listeners or viewers feel comfortable is of paramount importance if you want to turn them into fans.

I remember listening to the radio in one city where a commercial came on for an appliance store. I learned later that it was a family-owned business, and the man in the commercial had been running the store for decades, and that the little girl in the commercial with him was his granddaughter. I also learned that she had been in the commercials with him for a few years, and even starred with him in the TV commercials.

I learned all of that later, after I mentioned to someone having heard this bizarre ad with an old man and a little girl.

All the cuteness of the radio commercial was lost on me, because I didn't know the backstory. I had no idea who these people were, didn't understand their cutesy little inside jokes, and really had no idea why they were there.

So for that moment, I was the person coming back from the bathroom feeling uncomfortable that I didn't know what was going on.

There are ways to bridge those gaps. If the little girl had simply referred to the man as "Grandpa", I could have made the connection, and the word would have taken three-quarters of a second to say, so it wouldn't have diluted the message.

In my video series, I usually acknowledge that I have given the backstory before, saying, "If you're new to the show, my name is Neil, and..." before I give a brief history of what the show is about, and where it's headed. I make sure it's short enough so as to avoid being tiresome for the handful of people who *do* watch every episode, but descriptive enough that the show makes sense.

If you're doing a show, and one of your co-host looks at you, says, "good thing it wasn't broccoli", and then everyone laughs, I'm going to wonder what's so funny about broccoli, or you run the risk of me feeling uncomfortable enough that I tune out. So find a quick and easy way to clue me in, or lean on broccoli as a punch line a little less often.

Platforms and Promotion

Once your show is out in the world, of course, the next task is to find ways to let people know it's there.

If you've purchased this book, my guess is that your network doesn't have a seven-figure advertising budget and a marketing department of six people tasked full-time with getting you a bigger audience.

Often, you're the only one at the controls in these situations, and that can be daunting.

You're not alone, there. In fact, this chapter might be a little shorter than some of the others because I haven't found a bullet-proof solution for the one-man-bands and solopreneurs that I can lay out for you here. I'm still working on a variety of solutions myself, including having invested hundreds of hours into writing a computer program that will help automate some of the process for me.

And "automate" is the word that should trigger some concern, if you've been following my admonitions about making genuine connections.

Connecting with other people has always been viewed as important – it's why we got that steady diet of weepy TV commercials through the 1970s where a son would call a tearful Mom to wish her a Happy Mothers' Day and extol the virtues of the latest long distance plan from the phone company, who just wanted to keep us all connected.

When Facebook came along, people flocked to the platform because it would allow us to reconnect with people we'd lost touch with. For plenty of people, it didn't take long to recognize the reasons why we let those connections go in the first place. But even bi-coastal or trans-global marriages came about because of what started as virtual connections.

Then what I like to think of as the darker side of those connections started to take root. Not dark in a sinister sense, although there's plenty of that out in the world as well, but do you remember Klout Scores? Klout was a service – more of a disservice, really – that started in 2008 and would assign you a score from 1 to 100 based on the quality of your connections. At least, that was the idea. But in reality, "quality" wasn't really part of the equation. Mostly, you were given a high Klout score if you were connected to a lot of other people. (The only Klout score in history of 100, by the way, was given to Justin Bieber.) It's because of Klout scores that we now have social media influencers – and that wonderful subset of social media influencers who have contributed nothing to the world and achieved nothing in their lives except a high follower count.

I saw, and briefly followed, one guy on Twitter who billed himself as a social media expert specializing in building connections. He had a follower count in the six figures and I thought to myself, well, that many people can't *all* be wrong, so I followed.

Within 24 hours, I had received 177 tweets from this one person. Every one of them was a link to either an article or a video on his website. Each of those was basically an instructional piece on how to automate a lot of your social media, and how to build a huge audience without having to invest much time.

In that same 24-hour period, this expert on connection-building didn't have a single interaction with any of his six-figure follower count. Didn't like anything. Didn't retweet anything. Didn't respond to anyone. Didn't have any conversations. So this guru apparently still lives in the Klout score era, where other people are simply seen as the means to an end.

Rather than simply stand and throw stones, though, let's examine our own use of connections and see if they pass the sniff test.

If I'm a fan of your podcast – is there an easy way to get in touch with you or your team, or ask a question?

If I reach out to your show or your company on social media, will someone respond? And maybe respond without cutting and pasting text from the "Officially Approved Interaction Scripts" document?

While we're on the subject of the officially approved scripts, I know I'm not the only person in the world *this* has happened to: I decided to switch cell phone providers. For the sake of the story, let's change the name to protect the guilty, and pretend I was using ACME Wireless (the same company Wile E. Coyote was using). So I called, went through the process, and at the end of the call, the person said, "Is there anything else I can do for you today?" No. The reason I called is because I'm severing the relationship. And then they said, "Thanks for choosing ACME!" That's how they ended the call where I canceled their service. By thanking me for choosing them. Either the script told them to say that, or they switched to autopilot and ended every call that way. Whichever answer is true, it's just more evidence that you don't care.

The guy who did his social media on autopilot did have one thing tangentially correct: There's a vast array of tools available to make it easier than ever to interact with your customers and fans. And that means it's a bigger sign than ever before that you just don't care, if you don't find a way to maintain a connection with me once you've gotten what you wanted.

Faking connection might work if what you're after is a one-night stand. But it's no way to build a fan base. And what I can almost guarantee you is that someone out there is doing it better.

So ultimately, my guidance on a social media presence and marketing platforms is this: Be in every place you possibly can.

However, that's only the first part of the sentence. The second part is critically important, because the full sentence is this: Be in every place you possibly can, even if that means automation, but be certain to respond to every potential fan who wants to actually have a conversation with you, and have actual engagements with others. Participate.

Yes, every platform will have stone-throwers and people who are simply there to be jerks and get attention. Trolls are everywhere. But spamming me with another link every 37 minutes and never responding to me is simply going to get you "un-followed", or even worse, blocked. Somewhere in all those comments and replies are people who could become genuine fans. Or maybe they're fans already who will spend the next three days telling everyone they know about how incredible it was that the host of their favorite show took the time to reply to a question they asked on social media. Yes, people brag about that stuff. But they're just as quick to lose interest in someone who doesn't care that they're out there.

Do A Collaboration With... Yourself

There are tons of people in the podcast space and beyond, who are lauding cross-promotions and collaborations as the Holy Grail of what is essentially free marketing. The idea is this: Find a show you really like, a show whose audience you think will also like *your* show, and find a way to do an episode or project with them that will expose your show to their fans.

Heck, even *Star Trek* did this recently when characters from their animated series, *Lower Decks,* showed up as live humans in an episode of another *Trek* series, *Strange New Worlds*.

Here comes the curve ball, however: Are you doing any collaborations or cross-promotions with yourself?

If you're talking about a subject in today's show that you also mentioned last week, are you mentioning that prior coverage and telling me where I can find it? If you're doing a radio morning show and on today's show, you made a reference to The Rolling Stones, did you remember to mention that your station has a Rolling Stones special that runs every Saturday afternoon at 4? If your co-host is talking about her new puppy that she adopted from the Humane Society, is there a blog post on the station's website where fans can go see photos of the puppy, with a link to the Humane Society's website, and are you promoting that blog entry on the air? Will the midday host come on in a few hours and make a quick mention that the studio smells like wet dog today because so-and-so from the morning show celebrated Bring Your Dog To Work Day, and you should see the adorable photos, which you can get to on the station's Facebook page?

If you're recording episode 47 of your podcast, and you're expanding on something you said in a previous episode, are you at least mentioning that episode, if not linking to it in your show notes? For example, "We've talked before on the show about how numerous studies demonstrate melatonin supplements don't really do much to help most people sleep and if you missed that episode, it's on our website at..."

Recycle as much as possible. If you've covered something before, make it easy to find, and then send people to it. Dave Jackson from *The School of Podcasting* has mastered this skill. He'll talk about a subject he has mentioned before, and he'll send you to a specific link that's simply the episode number of the show where he mentioned it - something as simple as saying, "We talked a few weeks ago about this subject on Episode 43 of the show and if you missed it, you can find the conversation at schoolofpodcasting.com/43."

Make the place they're going to go as easy as possible to find. In fact, it's tempting to give this point its own chapter, because it's that important.

Don't assume that the person listening is sitting there with Notepad open on their computer, or with a pen and paper in their hand just in case you had some wisdom that needed to be written down for later use. Don't send them to "mywebsite.com/subfolder/nestedsubfolder/title-with-hyphens-and-seven-which-might-be-a-word-or-is-it-the-numeral-7". Send them to "mywebsite.com/puppy". Ask your web people how to do that, or install a plugin that will do it for you.

Create recyclable content. Give it a home that's easy to find. Tell people where to find it and send them there. And once they're there, make sure there's *other* recyclable content they might *also* be interested in. And open the links in new tabs so they don't lose the place they were in originally.

Do Things On Purpose

Defensibility – a word we may very well have just coined here – is the art of doing things on purpose. It's what separates the pros from the cons and by that, I don't mean what separates the positives from the negatives.

By one of its more strict definitions, the moment you get paid for something, you're a professional. The word "professional" also conveys, at least to some people, a certain standard. of performance. A professional athlete is likely better at their sport than an amateur, for example. Same for a professional versus an amateur guitarist. Or chef. There's the implication that the professional is just plain better at what they do. But regardless of your field of endeavor, the moment somebody writes you a check, you're expected to bring your A-game. And that's where "doing things on purpose" comes into play.

Ideally, professionals are *always* bringing their A-game. To me, that's the responsibility you assume when you *accept* the check. But that assumption is not, as it turns out, universal.

If you're being paid to provide a service, doing things on purpose means that every choice that was made on a specific project was made deliberately, and with consideration. And that if it came down to it, you'd be able to defend every one of those choices and explain the rationale behind them. If that's not true, then you've abdicated your responsibility as a professional, and your client has wasted their money.

Recently in the middle of a big-market morning show I was working with, I heard a commercial with three voices in it, playing characters in a made-up scenario. And guess what? Every single one of them had a name. And the more I thought of it, the more I realized it's been ages since I heard a commercial with characters in it, where they weren't assigned arbitrary names. Were the writers and producers doing things on purpose when they gave time-consuming names to these characters in this 30-second play? What specific purpose did the names serve? And why were the names they chose as white as the snow in the Rockies?

MAN 1: Hey Bob!

MAN 2: Yeah, Jim?

MAN 1: What are you doing?

They could have completely skipped the part where they made up names for the characters that served no purpose, and instead devoted those 3 seconds to doing a better job advertising the business.

When we pay money to our doctors, our lawyers and our mechanics, we assume that it's because they're going to bring their A-game, and do a proper job that's informed by proper training and comprehensive knowledge about what paths will lead to the best possible outcomes for us. But shouldn't that be true of everybody that gets paid to do something? If you're bagging my groceries, I want to know why you chose to put the loaf of bread on the bottom of the bag under the bottle of soda. Is there a reason? Or do you just not care about anything today?

It's surprising how many people could be choosing to do things on purpose who instead fall back on phrases like, "that's just how we've always done it". If there's a defensible reason for having always done it that way, then let stakeholders and team members know, so they'll better understand the process and go forward with the confidence that things are done by design.

Clients who rely on me for production of their radio commercials, and students who've enrolled in my copywriting course, know only too well how I feel about music beds in advertising. Does it serve a purpose? No? Then get it out of there. If the purpose of the music bed is to liven up the spot, maybe try writing copy that doesn't *suck*, and you won't *need* the music bed. Same for you, radio DJ who plays music in the background of their conversations to help it feel like things are moving along. Maybe you should try having conversations that are *actually* moving along.

Every sentence in an advertisement should serve a purpose. Every music track in a podcast should have been a deliberate choice, and the producer should be able to describe why *this* track instead of *that* one.

Every ingredient in my entree should be there for a reason. Every time the ball leaves the pitcher's hand, it should be to throw the pitch that the catcher decided was the best one to throw now, and here's why.

Doing things on purpose is what defines a pro. The opposite of a pro is either an amateur, or a con.

The Fear of Being Different

I mentioned it in the last chapter, but let me expand on it here: "Because we've always done it that way," is a lousy reason to do anything. So is "because everybody else does it."

The second one is the reason why most podcasts have music at the beginning, under the introduction. The music is only there because everybody else uses music, and the people behind various shows don't want to stray too far from the accepted norms.

Similarly, you'll see countless promotions for podcasts that include the phrase, "Get it wherever you get your podcasts." That phrase might win the prize for the most overused useless phrase in the history of promoting anything. It's meaningless. Imagine if *American Idol* ended their TV promos with "Get it wherever you watch your TV shows." Or if Coca-Cola said, "Get it wherever you get stuff to drink." If they did, we'd laugh at their incompetence. But podcasters do it by the hundreds, "because everybody else does it."

A few brave souls have even made up completely bogus reasons for the validity of such a ridiculous phrase, in arguments that hold water just as well as cheesecloth.

If you're on the Olympic rowing team, then there absolutely is an argument for doing things the way everybody else does it. In fact, your ability to do things the way everybody else does it probably dictates whether you make the team in the first place.

If "Olympic Synchronized Swimmer" is *not* what it currently says on your LinkedIn bio, however, it's worth examining whether the way "everybody else does it" is taking you away from the things that make you unique.

Recall the television show I referenced earlier, *24*. It was groundbreaking because the show happened in real-time. That is to say that five minutes on the show took five minutes to show on TV. If one of the characters got on a plane for a flight that would take two and a half hours, then for the next two and a half episodes, that character was stuck on a plane. They didn't get on a plane, then the show would cut away for a commercial break and when they came back from the commercial three minutes later, the flight had landed. If the commercial break lasted three minutes, then when the show came back it was three minutes later on the show. It was trailblazing and everyone was talking about it because it had never been done before. I'm sure that at some point, someone at the network must have said, "Well, that's not how everybody else does it." Thankfully, no one responsible for actually putting the show together paid any attention.

One podcasting client I worked with does a show about beer. When we had a conversation about things he could do to promote his show, I suggested doing every show as a live broadcast on YouTube, and either creating an ongoing partnership with one local brewery that would host the show, or going on a brewery tour where he'd be in a different location every week. Do the show live on YouTube, but release the audio recording every week as a podcast episode. It came across as a new idea simply because that's not how everybody else does it. People tend to record their shows at home where the podcast gurus have convinced them they will have the required control over the recording environment, then tightly edit them and release them when they are pristine.

...except that in the case of beer enthusiasts, that's not how they're used to having conversations. They're used to having them in noisy bars, talking to the brewmasters and bartenders and reacting in real-time to the various things going on at the table or in the venue.

It's a perfect example of how being different would actually result in a better, more authentic show that was more comfortable for the audience to listen to.

If your podcast is about fixing cars, why not do the show from an auto repair shop? Let's hear the noises in the background that everybody else believes simply pollutes the audio quality.

I was notorious during the on-air phase of my radio career for taking the morning show out on the road and doing it from various locations in the city. Heck, we even did "Live On The Lawn" shows that were done in the area in front of the building, just because it was different and interesting. At one station, we had to purchase equipment and put systems in place to pull those broadcasts together, because “nobody else does it that way”. To me, that was an even better reason to do it.

One time, we offered contest winners a limousine ride to work as one small part of a prize we gave away for Administrative Professionals Week. Everyone else in town would just give away something like that as a prize, announce the winner’s name and be done with it. Instead, we did the morning show live from the limousine while we were driving to pick up the winner. It gave us all kinds of options for doing things we didn’t normally get to do, including literally having the morning show stuck in traffic while doing the traffic reports from the highway where the big jam was happening.

Remember my friend who talked about the nine stations in town fighting over the same Kelly Clarkson hit, and think about the potential value of being the one station that plays the B-sides instead.

Leverage the Recording Studio in Your Pocket

Natural sound has always been a fascination for both listeners and producers of spoken word audio content. Replicating sounds and effects that only happen in nature can be both challenging and rewarding when done right, and irritating when done wrong.

In radio's Golden Age, creating sound effects was done on the fly, often using intricate gadgetry that took hours to build for an effect that would only last a few seconds.

Of course, technology has completely changed our approach to natural sound. But don't get ahead of me – it hasn't changed in the way you think.

Sure, with access to a library of sound effects, you can approximate the natural sound of all kinds of things. You can hear the waves lapping on the shore as a cruise ship passes and the seagulls make whatever that sound is that seagulls make (sorry, *Finding Nemo* has me forever hearing seagulls as saying, "Mine?"). What you can't replicate with digital tricks is the nuances of human speech, and in most cases, the differences in what things *sound* like when they're recorded in a natural setting versus a studio environment.

I recently heard a radio commercial where the announcer was capturing the excitement of a sale by jumping out of a plane. Excited, and shouting to be heard over the natural sound of the plane and the wind, they acted their way admirably through the script in the time allotted, and we moved on to the next commercial.

What a wasted opportunity.

Here's what I mean when I say that technology has changed our approach to natural sound – **it has made it easier for producers to be lazy**. There's no reason to have an announcer in a studio to read that commercial, having to pretend like they're jumping out of a plane, when technology has made it possible to more faithfully recreate the nuances that can bring a script to life.

Am I suggesting that you should have your announcer take the script on a sheet of paper and *actually* jump out of a plane? Of course not. But for exactly zero extra expense, I can pretty faithfully replicate those sounds with a little imagination.

Find a back road that you can drive down uninterrupted for a few seconds. 15 seconds or so should be enough. Have your announcer lean out the window and read the script while someone drives along – carefully – going at least 10 or 15 miles per hour. If it works better, have the announcer face the *back* of the vehicle to cut down some of the wind noise.

Know what you get then? Natural sound. You get *actual* wind buffeting an *actually* excited announcer who's having their breath taken away, just like it would if they were skydiving.

Know what most (lazy) producers would say about that approach? "The audio quality would be terrible."

You mean, the way it would be if someone were *actually* skydiving? If you're going to commit to the theater of the mind, then actually commit to it.

Voices sound different on a windy day than they do in a studio with wind sound effects playing. (If you want to get technical about it, not only do people project differently when they're speaking outdoors, but the outdoor environment also "steals" certain audio frequencies.)

A few seconds into the demo reel I use for voiceover work, you'll hear me reading a commercial and biting into an apple, then continuing to talk with food in my mouth. At the session, the producer wanted to use an apple biting sound effect, and for me to *pretend* to have food in my mouth. Instead, we ran across the street and bought a couple of *real* apples from a convenience store. Good thing we bought two, because it took several takes before we got one that combined the right amount of crunch and mouth noise to make it sound realistic.

So why do you have an announcer, sitting in a chair, pretending to talk to us while they're out jogging? Unless your phone was built prior to 2010, it has a pretty decent microphone in it. A microphone that you can record on the free apps on your phone. Give your announcer a script, some Nikes and send them out to sound like an actual person who's actually jogging because... uh... they are. Again – bingo. Natural sound.

On a related note, let me tell you about what I think was the best Public Service Announcement that was ever done in the ongoing effort to curb drunk driving. It was done by the team at CHUM Radio in Toronto, and written by Mike Occomore. The message was to discourage people from drinking and driving, and Mike found a way to do it like no one else ever had. He took a group of half a dozen people into one of the station's recording studios, where they were given unlimited pizza, beer and wine. After a couple of hours, producer Al Campagnola pressed "Record" on the tape deck as the group continued to get completely hammered. Mike and Al then lifted several clips of the group trying to read various pieces of copy they'd been given. The listener heard a slobbering, screaming, drunken bunch of idiots, and a simple announcer tag said,

If this is how adults react behind a mike after a few drinks, imagine their reactions behind a wheel.

It was brilliant theater because all we were given was the natural sound of adults behaving badly. Suddenly, however, we were transported in our minds to the bad memory of every obnoxious drunk we'd ever had the misfortune of having to spend time with. The tag made its point brilliantly. And not surprisingly, the spot was held up as one of the best public service announcements produced anywhere in North America.

If the audio is effective, the listener's brain will construct whatever buildings, props and landscapes are needed to complete the scene.

Once you hear the spot, you immediately understand that using genuine drunk people instead of having actors pretend to be drunk is a huge part of what makes the spot work – especially when you're told at the beginning that what you're hearing is real. It provokes that same instinct that makes people slow down to look at a car accident, unable to avert their eyes.

As Orson Welles learned with *War of the Worlds*, there's no limit on where an audio-only medium can take the listener's imagination. In addition, most radio stations now have massive libraries of sound effects that can make any production sound even more realistic. Want your own, more authentic sound effects? Make them yourself. You want the spot for your car dealership to sound like it really happened in the mechanic's bay? Go to the dealer, take out your iPhone and hold it up in the air for two minutes. There you go, genuine sound. If you really want it to be authentic, record the voiceover there, too.

Natural sound doesn't have to be complicated. As a morning show host, I used to really look forward to the days when we would do a "random draw" for some big prize we were giving away. When draw time came, I would grab the trash can from under the mixing console, put it beside my microphone and talk directly into the trash can. My exasperated co-host would explain that I had crawled inside the draw drum again, and I would hand them the winning entry from deep inside the massive drum full of entries. On the air, it was an incredibly convincing effect – especially when I would knock over my chair on the way out, which made it sound like the drum had collapsed under my weight. Then the pause, the brief silence and the inevitable, "I'm okay!"

Orson Welles used 1938 technology and had people convinced that we were under alien attack through the skilled use of production techniques and great voice talent. Imagine what's achievable now! Especially if we work as hard at getting it right as Welles did, and think less about taking shortcuts to get it done faster.

How Do You Not Run Out of New Things to Say?

That line is from a great song, called "How Do You Keep The Music Playing", sung in 1982 by James Ingram and Patti Austin, and it's a question encountered by tons of broadcasters and podcasters alike.

The answer isn't as difficult as you think.

I'll give you a quick few examples that are tangentially related. Often, over the course of writing this book, I would set my laptop down and go for a walk. It wasn't so much to stretch my legs or to get the blood pumping again, it was for a simple change of scenery which, hopefully, would lead to a shift in perspective. Although I'd espoused that idea for decades before, it was brought home to me in the middle of COVID-19, when I was doing an interview with a neuroscientist who was on the show to talk about the challenges of setting up an effective home office.

For me, one of the great weaknesses of having an office at home is proximity to the fridge, the TV, the piano... all the things that could take me out of "work mode" and put me into a completely unproductive frame of mind. What this expert suggested - and it worked both then and now, every time I try it - was to leave the house every morning and go somewhere. Coffee shop, bakery, even just a drive around the block, it didn't matter what the destination was. The key was the return from the coffee shop, and walking in the house and heading straight to my desk, the way I would have done if my office were in some corporate office building instead of my basement. Something about the act of leaving and returning to a specific, different environment caused my brain to treat that new environment as if it were in some place other than my house. In essence, I was tricking my brain into thinking it was somewhere other than the room next to the piano. And that perspective can shine an entirely new light on your thought processes.

In my own case, because I teach an online course about copywriting, and because I work with radio hosts and podcasters, I also use the walk as an opportunity to find new things to talk about with those constituencies. Let's go through a quick list of things I could talk about on a radio show or podcast, based on the simple 20-minute walk to get downtown.

Down the street from my house, I found a restaurant called, "Thai Food Near Me". A few quick ideas that spring to mind:

- Best business names
- Leveraging Google search results
- Funniest names related to a job, like the dentist Dr. Payne

I walk past another restaurant that's a favorite among the tourists and always has a line down the street, and as I walk by I listen to the conversations the people in line are having. More ideas:

- Favorite restaurant
- Best meal I ever had
- Tourist spots in my town that I've never visited
- World's most beautiful accents

I get toward one of the many large-scale construction jobs happening downtown and I wonder what's playing in the AirPods of the person holding the sign that says, "Slow" on one side and "Stop" on the other.

- World's most boring jobs
- Worst spot in town for traffic jams
- Something the city should build
- Does anyone really go into the traffic cone business? Is there a "Traffic Cones R Us" store somewhere that I've just never seen? What other everyday things come from a place you've never seen them sold?

At the local toy store, ideas abound.

- Our generation's coolest toy
- A toy kids play with now that you just don't see the point of
- What's the coolest thing you ever found at a garage sale?
- What's something you should *never* buy used?
- What's the best deal you ever got on a used item?

Even the walk itself inspires ideas.

- Do you know anyone who has ever gotten a ticket for jaywalking?
- Have you ever walked up to a complete stranger and said something nice?

Election signs on the street made me think of these:

- Has your local elected representative ever contacted you in advance of a vote on an issue or a bill, to get your opinion?
- Who is the nicest celebrity you ever talked to for more than ten minutes?

And this one, that I think is gold:

- How did they come up with the idea for coffee? Think about it - that's pretty specific. One specific kind of bean. Not cocoa beans, pinto beans, kidney beans, no. The *coffee* bean. Then someone decided to *roast* it, *grind* it into a powder but it has to be a *coarse* powder because no, we're not going to dissolve it in water, we're going to pour water *over* it and drink the stuff that comes out the other side. How many failed iterations did that go through before we started charging nine dollars a cup for it?

That's twenty-one ideas for conversation starters, all from the simple act of taking a walk with both my eyes and my mind open. And those ideas were just skimming the surface of the first couple of things that came to mind. Each of those points probably has about ten or fifteen related ideas that could evolve from it if we tried hard enough.

If you're an interesting person, there is always interesting stuff to talk about. The only way that's *not* true is if you're either not bringing enough of yourself to the show (see Chapter 10), or too busy worrying about being an announcer to fully explore interesting things you could talk about (see Chapters 1 & 2).

Now, if we go back to the *Star Wars* podcast we've been talking about, I understand that your options for episode topics will be more limited. But you might be surprised how many ideas come flying at you when you just clear your head enough to give them a place to land.

Afterword

As I said at the outset, this book merely scratches the surface of what you might achieve with a coach who's able to work with you, one-on-one, to diagnose your specific issues and come up with fixes that work for your show in particular.

Coincidentally, I offer such coaching, and have been doing it for decades with broadcasters and podcasters alike, including some very famous names you know whose identities will remain secret for a couple of reasons: First, dropping a famous name tends to color people's impression of what the end product might sound like and that puts a great deal of pressure on both teacher and student. Second, I noticed an increase a few years ago in the number of hosts who preferred to keep our working relationship private, so I operate now as though there were a non-disclosure agreement in place for everyone I work with, and am happy to sign an NDA for any new client who seeks to make that approach official and binding.

Because you have the book, and because you've come this far, I'm even more excited for the chance to work with you because you will have at least considered some of the ground work that normally eats up a bunch of time with new clients. So with that in mind, I have a discount to offer. Here's how to claim it:

Simply send an email to *neil@knoppstudios.com* with the subject line, "SEND ME THE DISCOUNT!" I'll email you back with a discount code that is good for one-time use. Enter the code I send you at the checkout when you book a coaching session with me on our website at *knoppstudios.com/coaching*, and it will automatically be applied. There are options there for short, medium and long-term coaching. Not surprisingly, the longer we work together, the cheaper it gets... but not for the reason you might think.

Sure, it's a volume discount. But the truth is that the longer we work together, the easier it gets because we'll have a track record of things we've discussed, implemented and measured. There'll be a level of familiarity there to prevent swooping in and making changes that contradict something else you're already working on. It also builds in accountability over time on both ends of the partnership, as we measure the distance between where we are and the destination that we've agreed is what "success" looks like. (And don't worry, your discounted price will continue to be your price for as long as we work together.)

If you're still not sure what to expect, or have questions, just drop me a line at that same e-mail address above and let me know how I can help. I'm excited to see where we can take you.

Made in United States
North Haven, CT
04 November 2026

21736090R00065